COLORING AND ACTIVITY BOOK

JUMBO
HALLOWEEN

BENDON™

©2006
Bendon Publishing International, Inc.
Ashland, OH 44805
www.bendonpub.com

CONNECT THE DOTS!

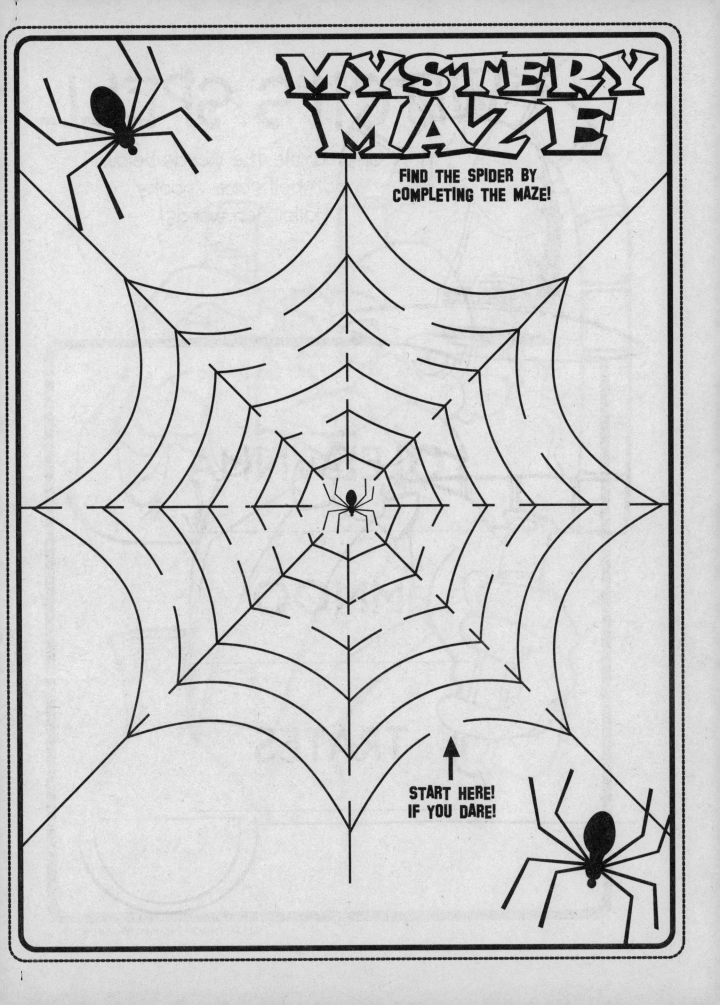

WITCH'S SPELL

Unscramble the words below
and spell some spooky
Halloween words!

LOLEEWNHA

_____

MNOO

_____

TRATES

_____

FINISH THE PICTURE.

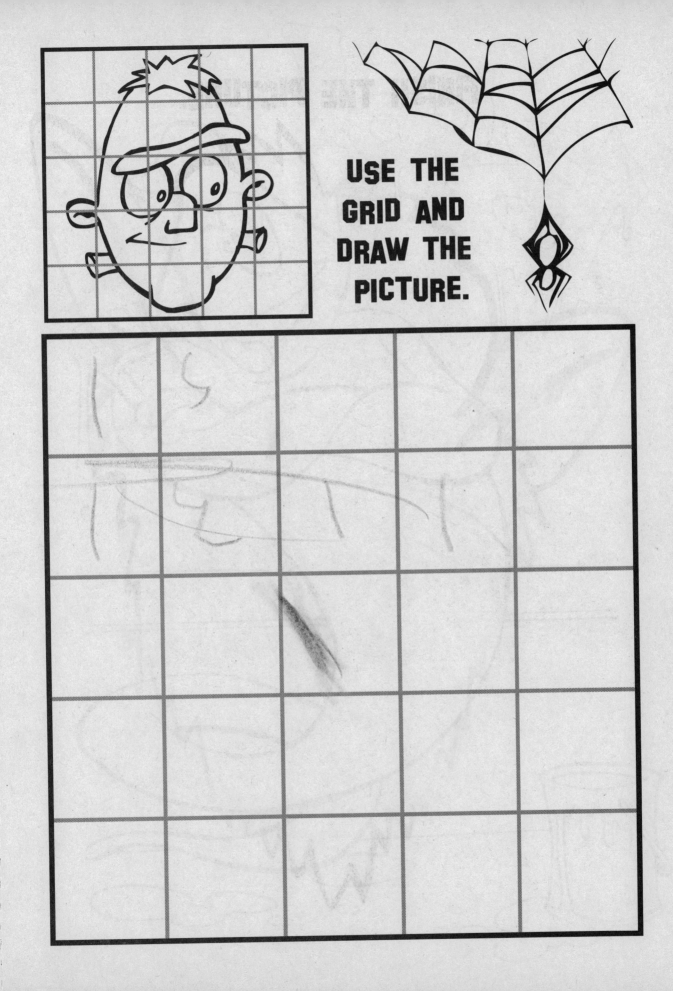

USE THE
GRID AND
DRAW THE
PICTURE.

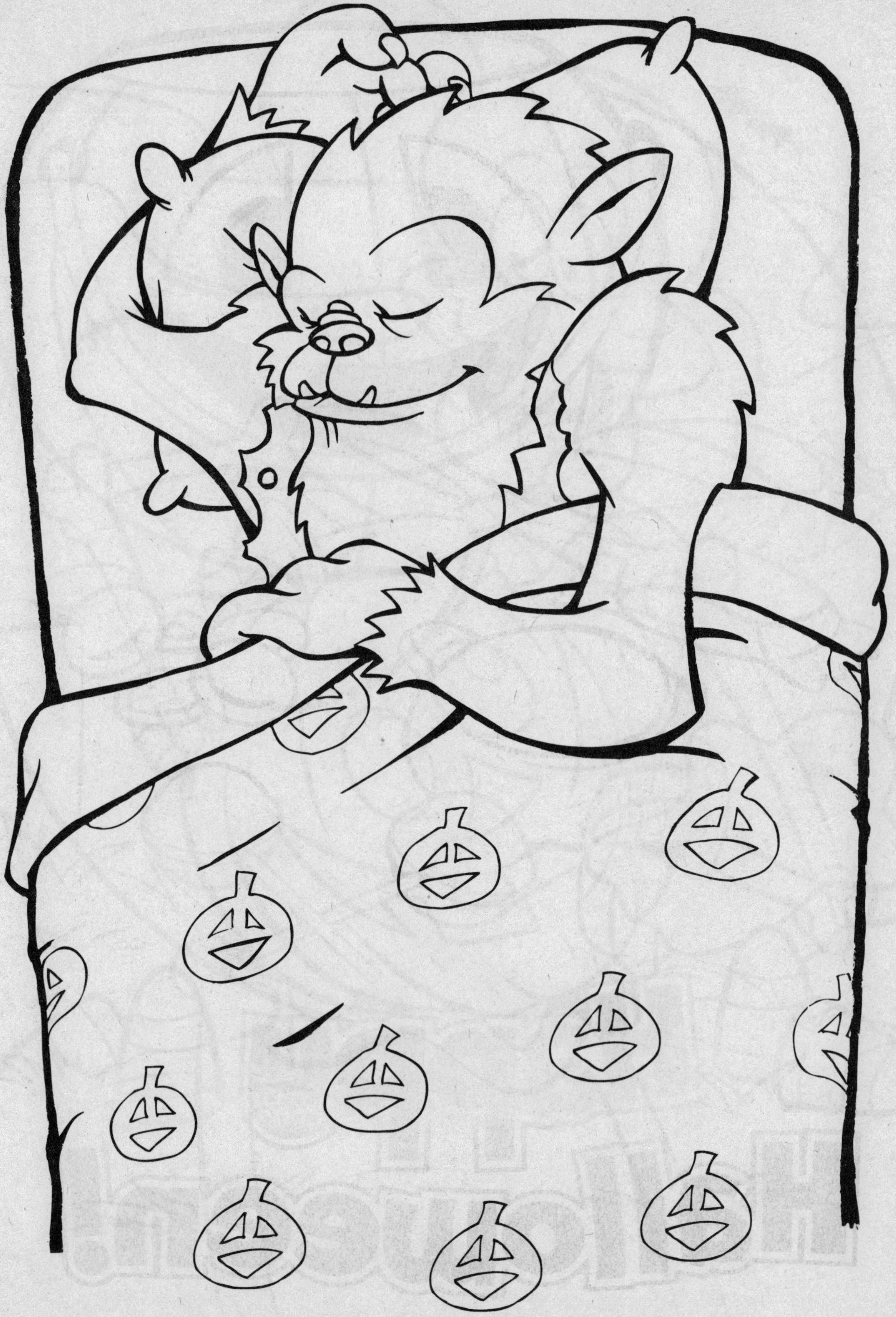

CONNECT THE DOTS!

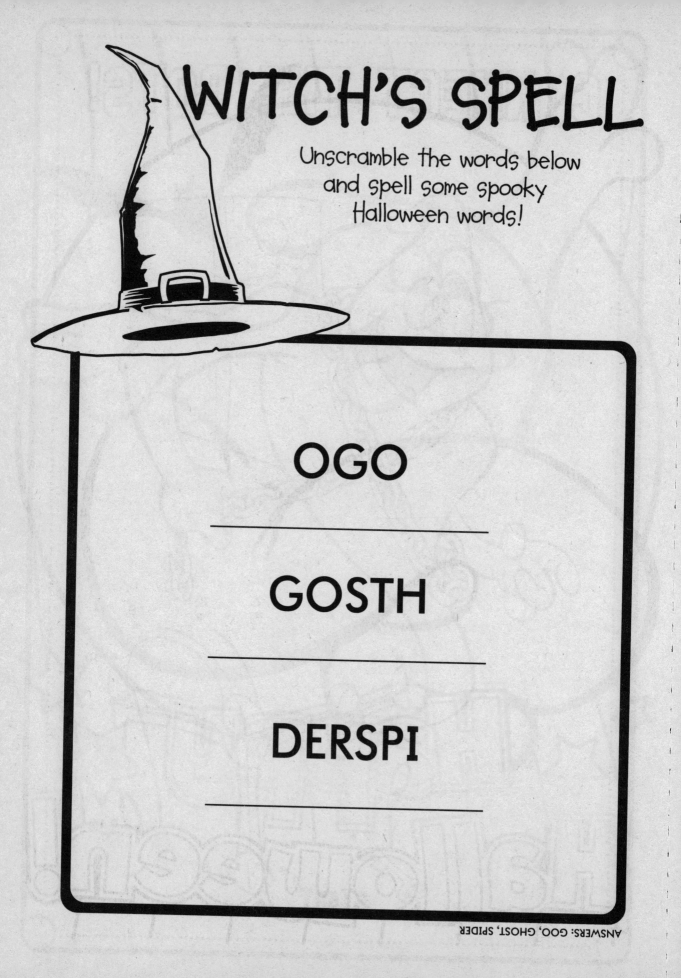

WITCH'S SPELL

Unscramble the words below
and spell some spooky
Halloween words!

OGO

_____

GOSTH

_____

DERSPI

_____

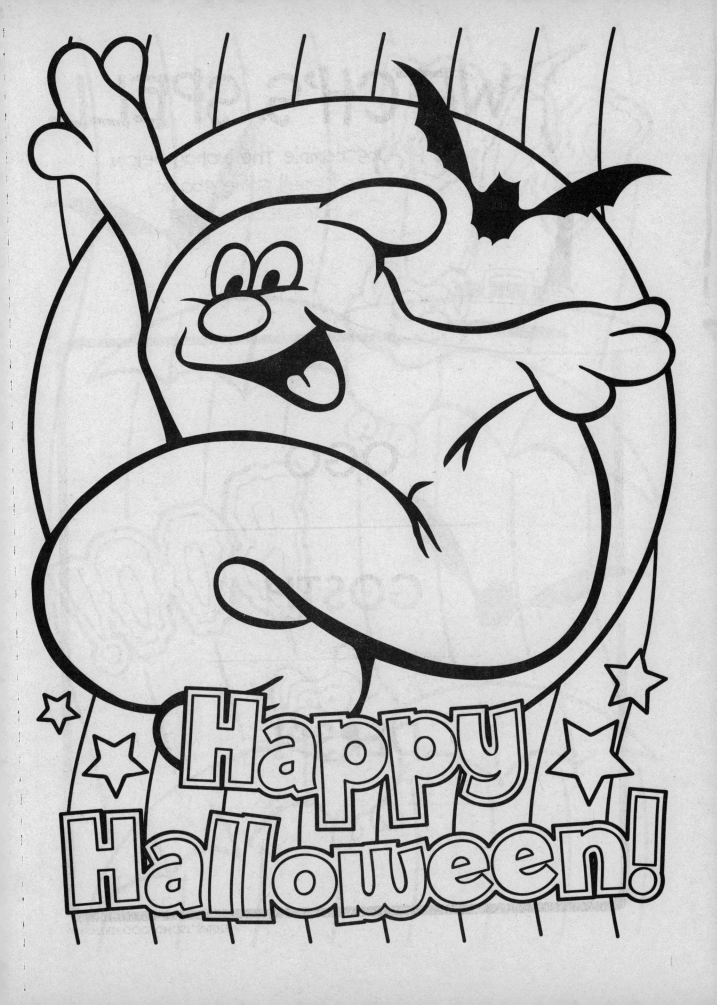

MAGIC MOBILE

Color the spooky pictures above. Then kindly ask an ADULT to help cut out the pictures and to follow the directions in making your very own MAGIC MOBILE!

STEP 1: Tie FOUR 6-inch pieces of ribbon OR string to the bottom of a coat hanger. Poke small holes through the tops of the PICTURES and attach them to the ends of the ribbon or string.

STEP 2: Hang your MAGIC MOBILE!

WHAT YOU NEED:
SCISSORS
STRING OR RIBBON
COAT HANGER

CONNECT THE DOTS!

START

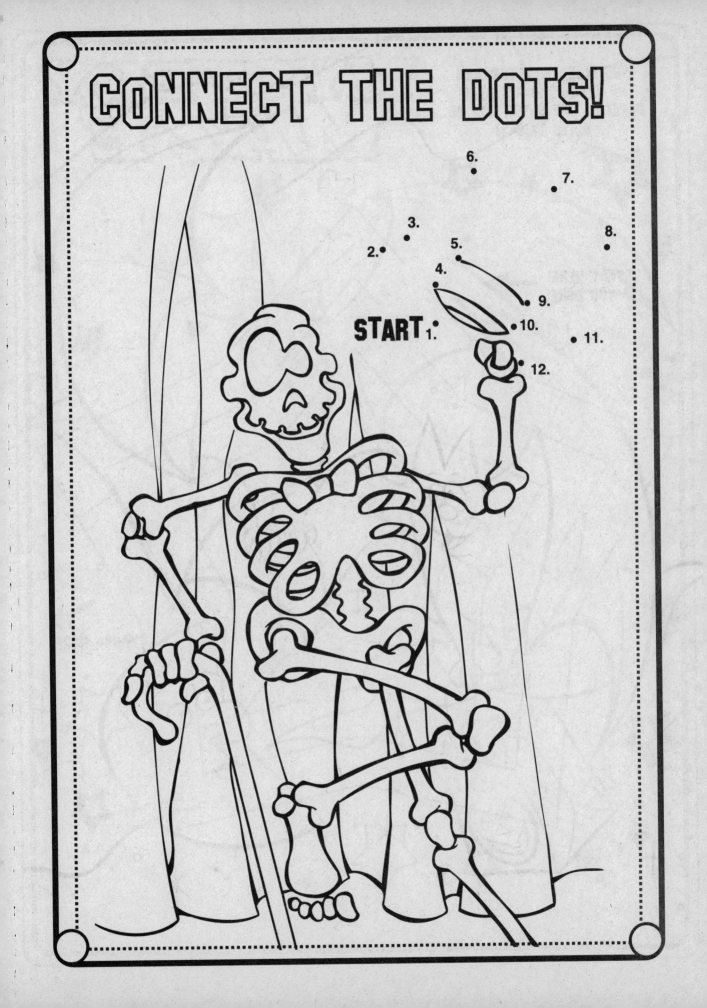

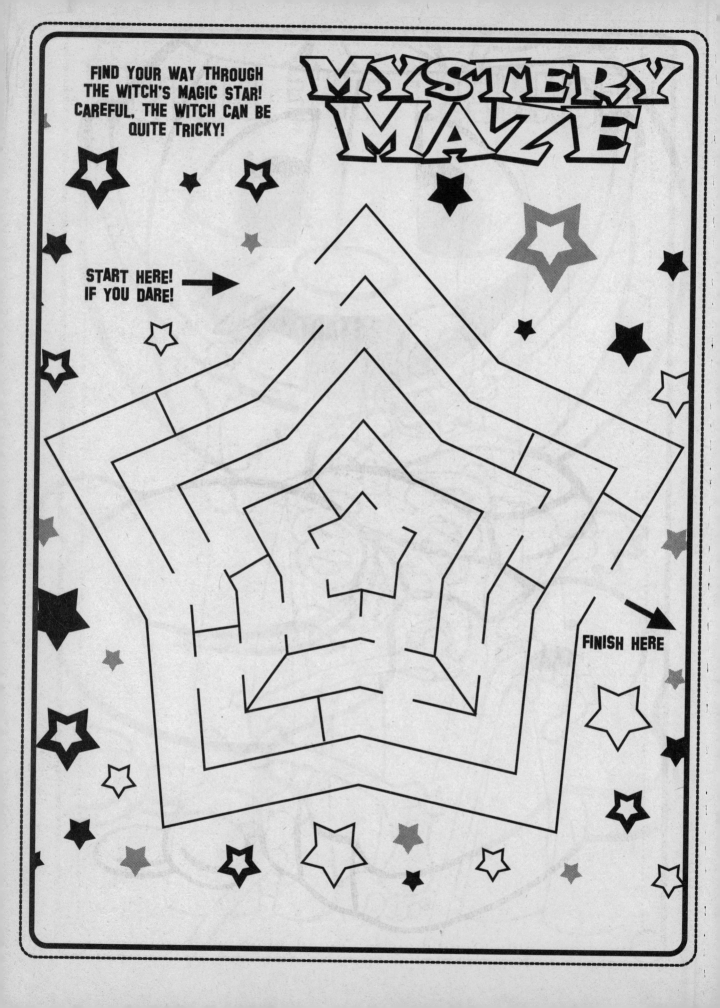

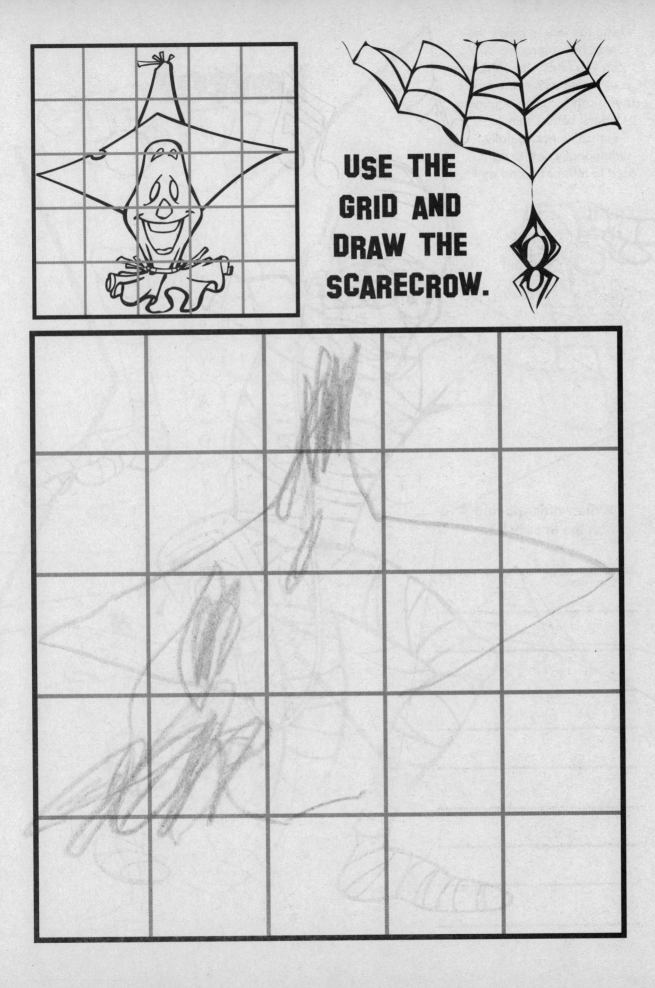

**USE THE
GRID AND
DRAW THE
SCARECROW.**

Using the letters inside the star, how many words can you find? The object is to create as many words as you can by using adjoining letters. Letters may join: vertically, horizontally, diagonally, left to right, right to left, or up and down.

EXAMPLE:

L	O	O	T	U	N
I	O	F	A	I	L
M	V	H	T	E	
E	F	G	E	R	A
E	I	L	O	A	D
R	T	E	G	U	Y

TOOL
OFF
RIGHT
TEAR
LOAD

Letter JuGGLe

T	O	O	R	U	N
I	H	F	A	L	L
M	I	F	F	T	Y
E	O	L	D	R	A
E	A	L	O	A	D
T	T	U	G	U	Y

Write words you find on the lines below!

_____
_____
_____
_____
_____
_____
_____
_____

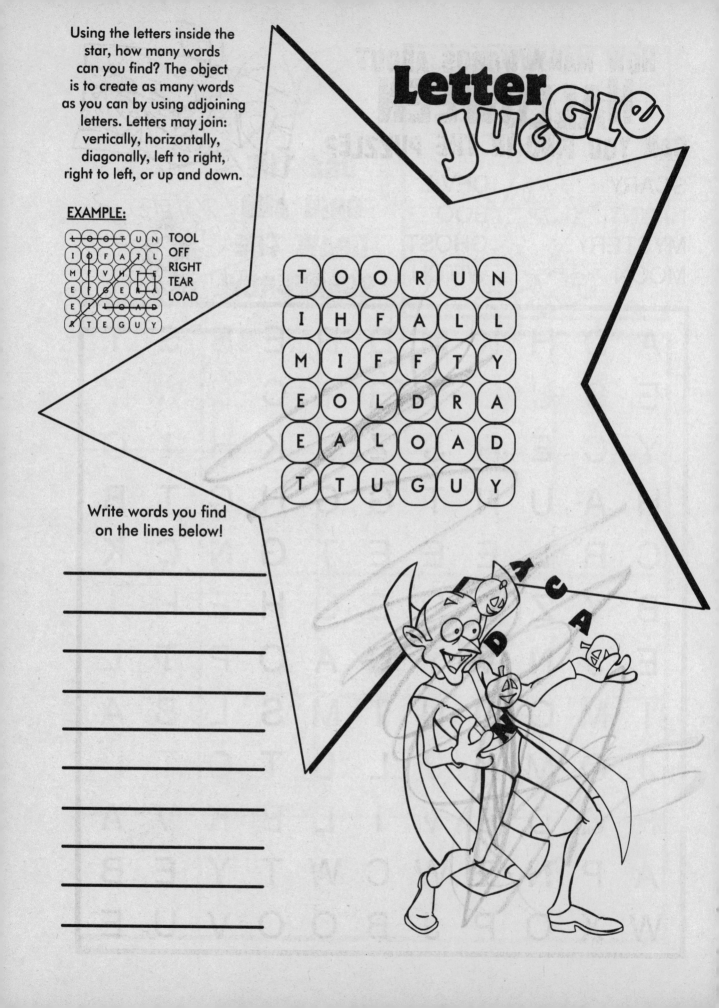

HOW MANY WORDS ABOUT
HALLOWEEN
CAN YOU FIND IN THE PUZZLE?

SCARY   DEVIL
HAUNT   BOO
MYSTERY   GHOST
MOON   WITCH

```
A D H K M D R E B S T
E S U O Y R I C R W Y
Y C E R S Z L K H I C
H A U N T G C H C T B
C R L E E E T G N C K
B Y Z C R E O H E H I
E J N V Y N A O P T L
I M O O N T M S L B A
J O M X J L L T O T U
P Q D E V I L B K V A
A P N E W C W T Y E B
W X O P J B O O V U E
```

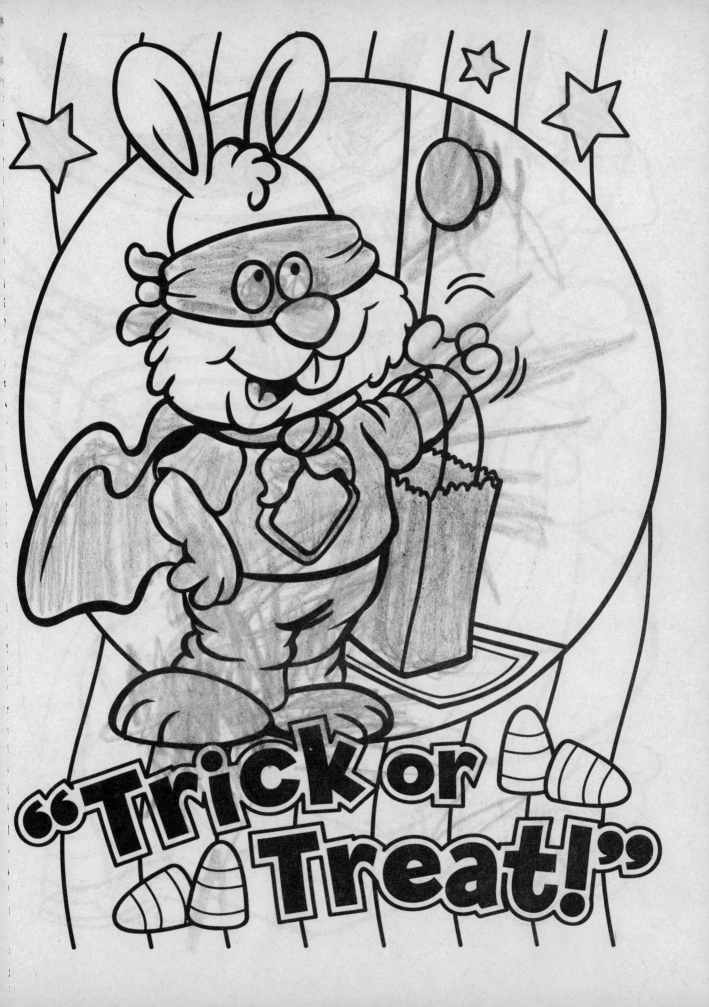

MAGIC MOBILE

BOO!

Color the spooky pictures above. Then kindly ask an ADULT to help cut out the pictures and to follow the directions in making your very own MAGIC MOBILE!

STEP 1: Tie FOUR 6-inch pieces of ribbon OR string to the bottom of a coat hanger. Poke small holes through the tops of the PICTURES and attach them to the ends of the ribbon or string.

STEP 2: Hang your MAGIC MOBILE!

WHAT YOU NEED:
SCISSORS
STRING OR RIBBON
COAT HANGER

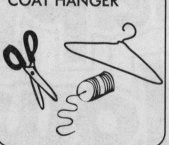

FINISH THE PICTURE.

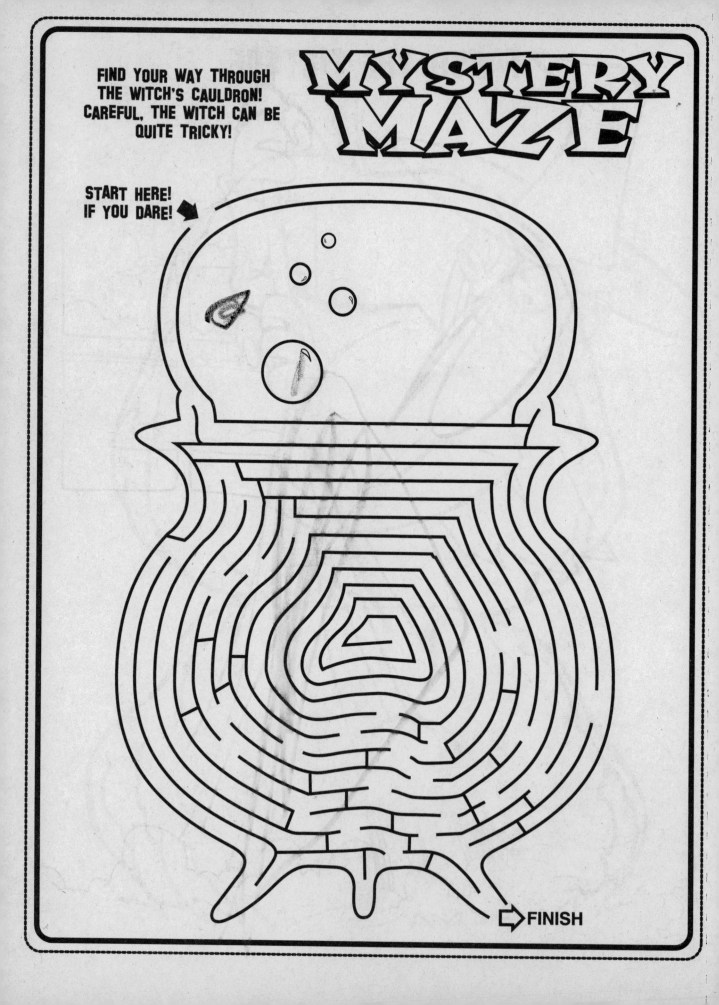

HOW MANY WORDS ABOUT
HALLOWEEN
CAN YOU FIND IN THE PUZZLE?

OCTOBER   GHOSTS
FALL   WITCHES
CANDY   HALLOWEEN
CORN   BOO

```
A D H K M D F E G S T
H A C A N D Y R H G Y
A R T O C T B M O F C
L K V M O G L H S R M
L F T H R N D E T I T
O A S O N F S B S G E
W L T W I T C H E S C
E L E L F R A U C T H
E O C T O B E R N A U
N A T P L H E A K T A
T N G R O A N G Y S B
L R B O O K A R B E C
```

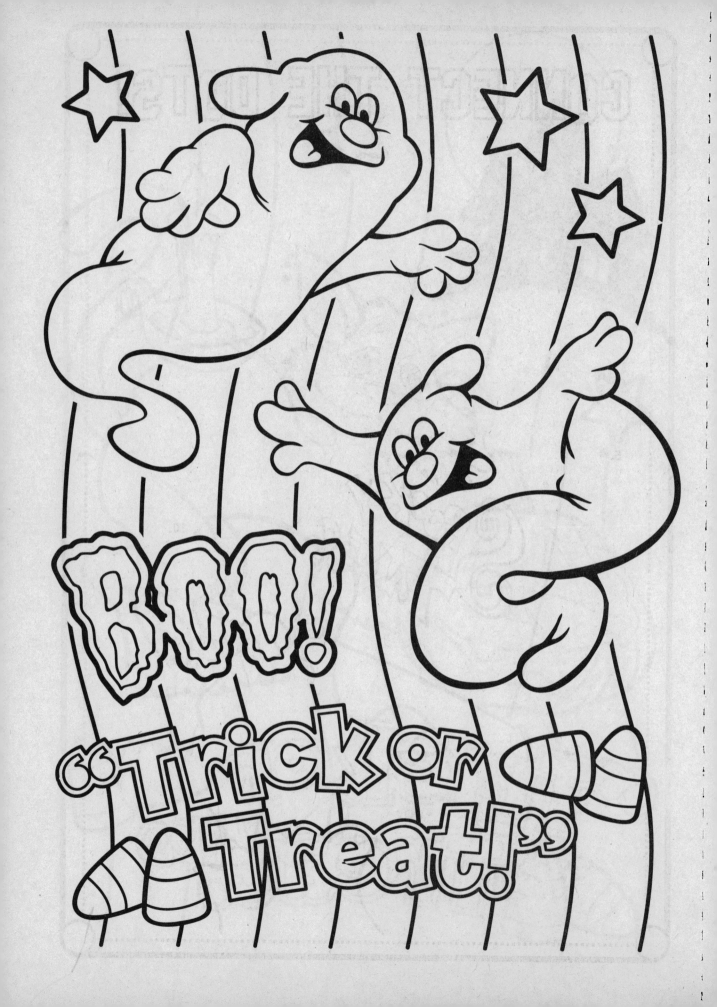

CONNECT THE DOTS!

FINISH THE PICTURE.

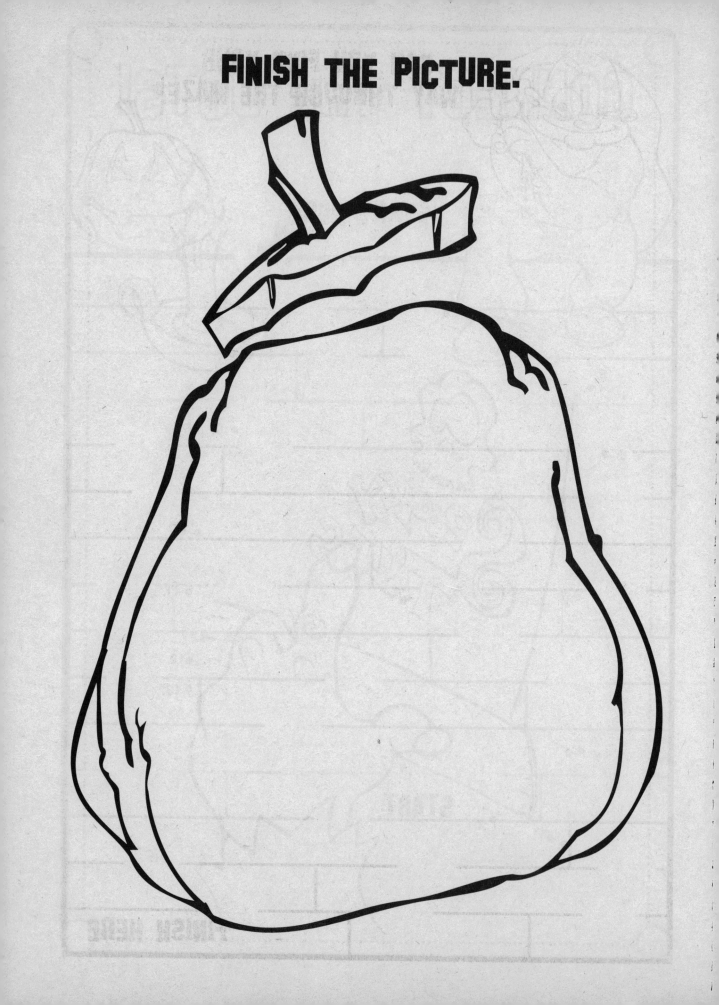

CAN YOU FIND YOUR WAY THROUGH THE MAZE?

START HERE

FINISH HERE

Using the letters inside the star, how many words can you find? The object is to create as many words as you can by using adjoining letters. Letters may join: vertically, horizontally, diagonally, left to right, right to left, or up and down.

Letter Juggle

EXAMPLE:

L O O T U N	TOOL
I O F A I L	OFF
M F V H E S	RIGHT
E F G E L T	TEAR
E R L O A D	LOAD
R T E G U Y	

T	O	O	L	S	B
E	H	F	A	Y	U
L	I	F	D	T	Y
L	E	N	D	R	A
S	A	L	A	D	R
C	T	U	G	C	N

Write words you find on the lines below!

_____
_____
_____
_____
_____
_____
_____
_____
_____

CONNECT THE DOTS!

START

12. • 1. •

2. •

11. • 3. •

10. • 4. •

9. • 5. •

8. • 7. • 6. •

FINISH THE PICTURE.

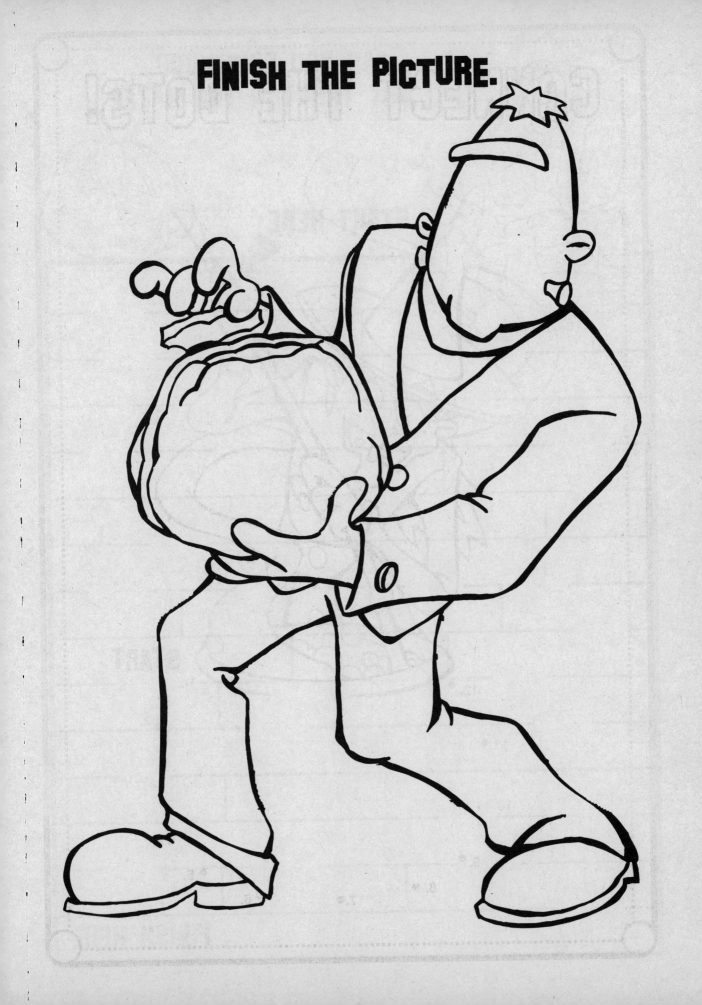

Using the letters inside the star, how many words can you find? The object is to create as many words as you can by using adjoining letters. Letters may join: vertically, horizontally, diagonally, left to right, right to left, or up and down.

Letter JuGGle

EXAMPLE:

EXAMPLE:

L	O	O	T	U	N
I	O	F	A	I	L
M	F	V	H	E	
E	F	G	E	R	A
E	I	L	O	A	D
R	T	E	G	U	Y

TOOL
OFF
RIGHT
TEAR
LOAD

W	O	O	L	S	C
E	I	O	M	A	N
L	A	N	O	T	V
L	E	R	D	R	A
S	T	A	N	D	R
C	T	S	W	A	Y

Write words you find on the lines below!

_____
_____
_____
_____
_____
_____
_____
_____

CONNECT THE DOTS!

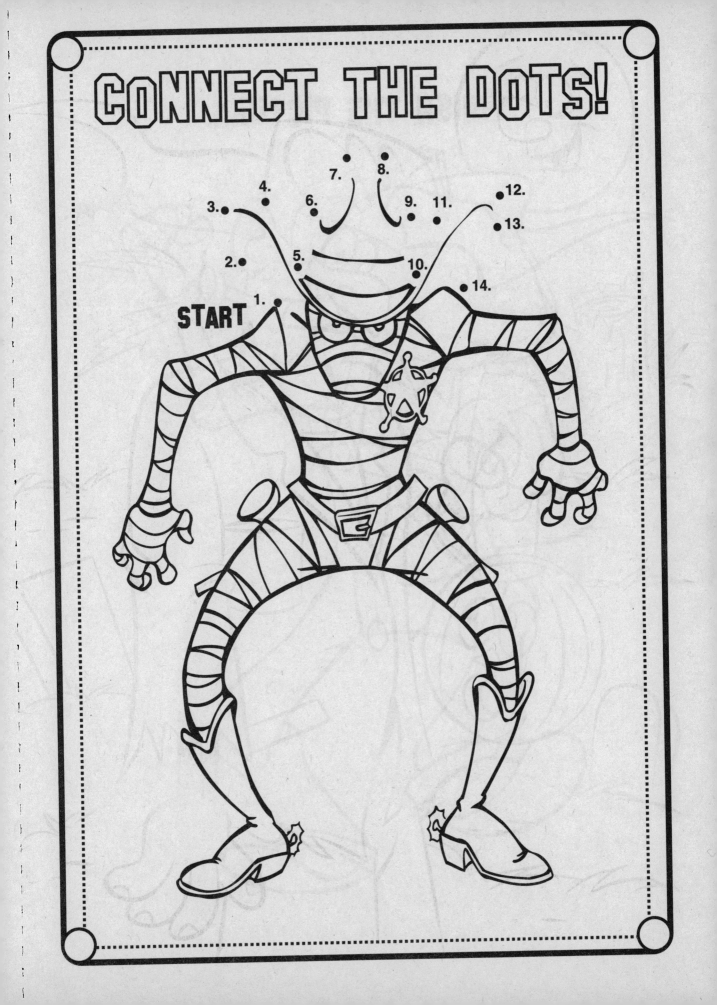

FINISH THE PICTURE.

MAGIC MOBILE

Color the spooky pictures above. Then kindly ask an ADULT to help cut out the pictures and to follow the directions in making your very own MAGIC MOBILE!

STEP 1: Tie FOUR 6-inch pieces of ribbon OR string to the bottom of a coat hanger. Poke small holes through the tops of the PICTURES and attach them to the ends of the ribbon or string.
STEP 2: Hang your MAGIC MOBILE!

WHAT YOU NEED:
SCISSORS
STRING OR RIBBON
COAT HANGER

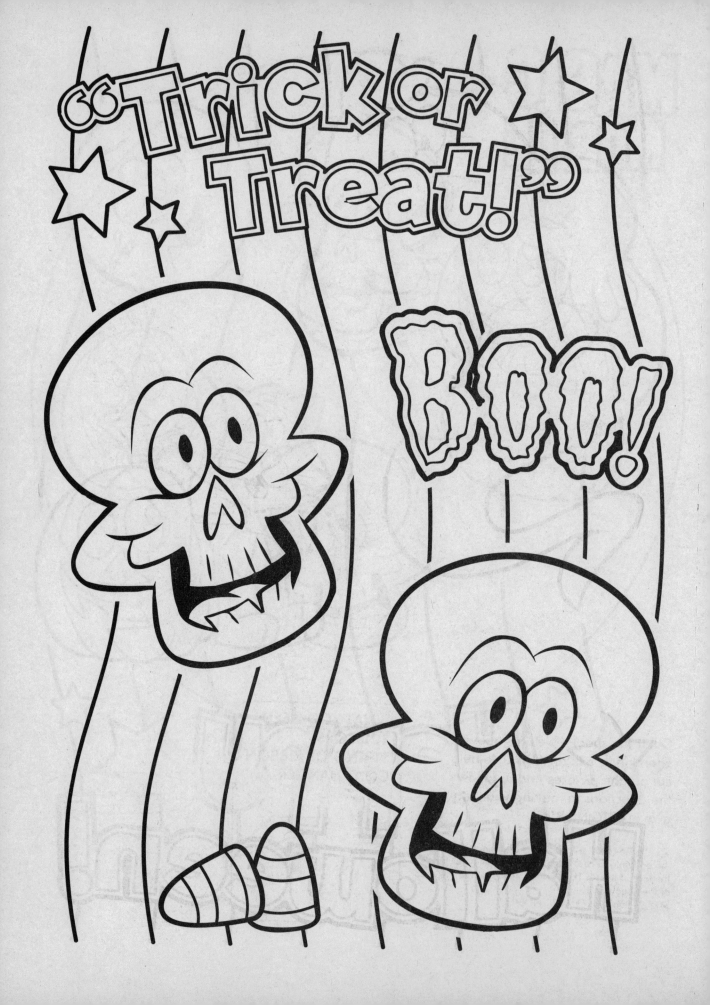

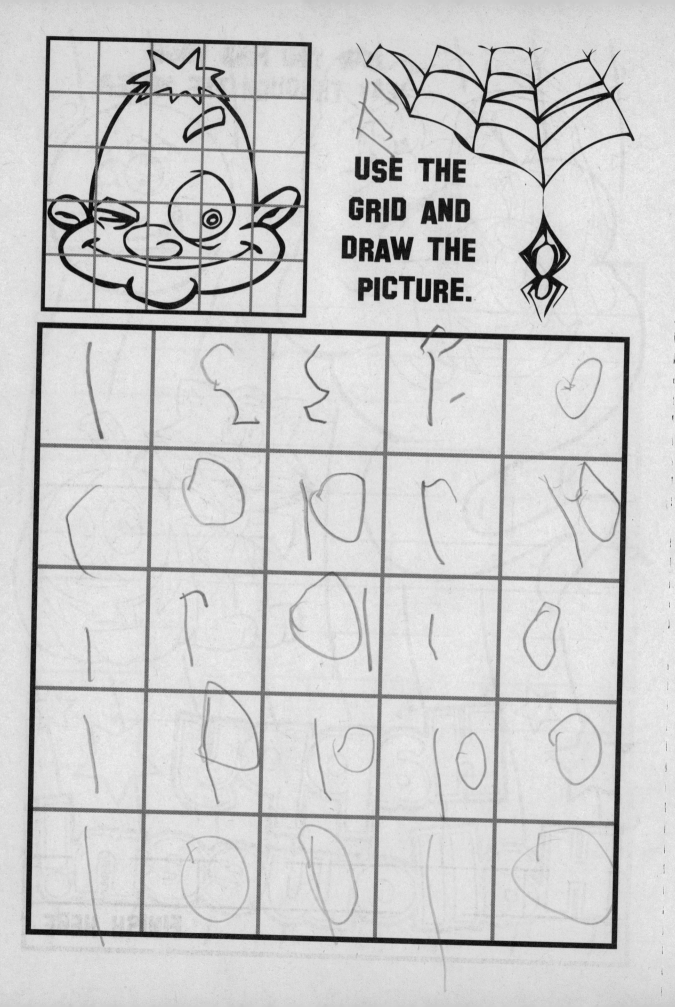

USE THE
GRID AND
DRAW THE
PICTURE.

CAN YOU FIND YOUR WAY THROUGH THE MAZE?

START HERE

FINISH HERE

HOW MANY WORDS ABOUT
HALLOWEEN
CAN YOU FIND IN THE PUZZLE?

CANDY

HARVEST

PUMPKIN

CAT

OWL

TREATS

BOO

CIDER

A D H K M D R E B S T

C S A O Y C I D E R Y

A C R R S Z L K H E C

N A V N T G C H C T B

D T E E T R E A T S K

Y Y S C R E O H E M L

E J T V Y N A O P T I

I P U M P K I N L B A

J O M X J L L T O O U

P Q D E V O W L K O A

A P N E W C W T Y E B

W X O P J K E T B U E

WITCH'S SPELL

Unscramble the words below
and spell some spooky
Halloween words!

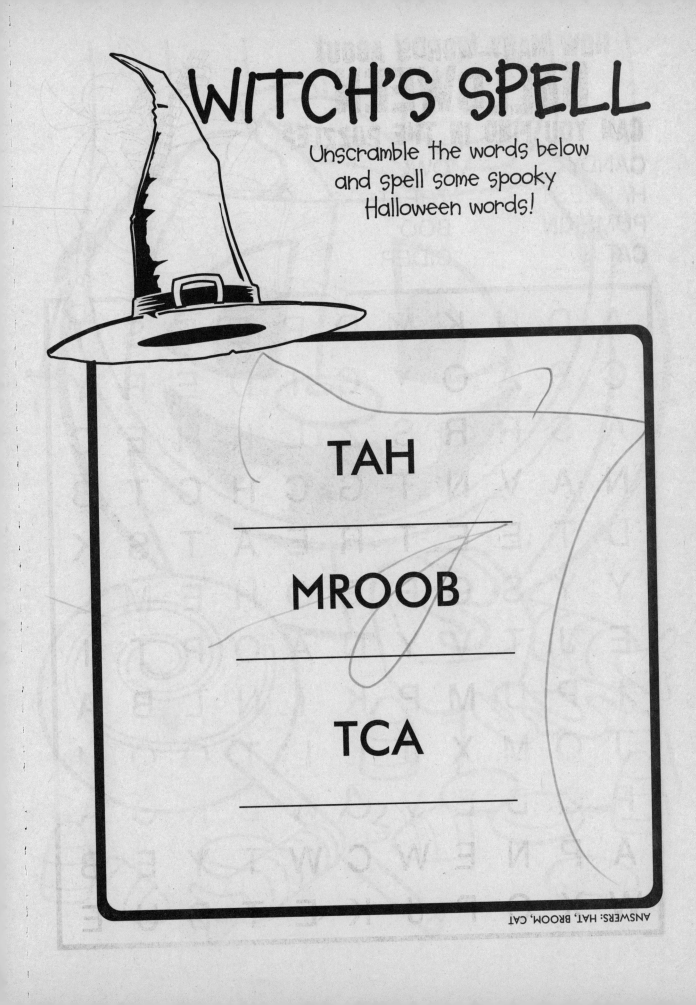

TAH

_____

MROOB

_____

TCA

_____

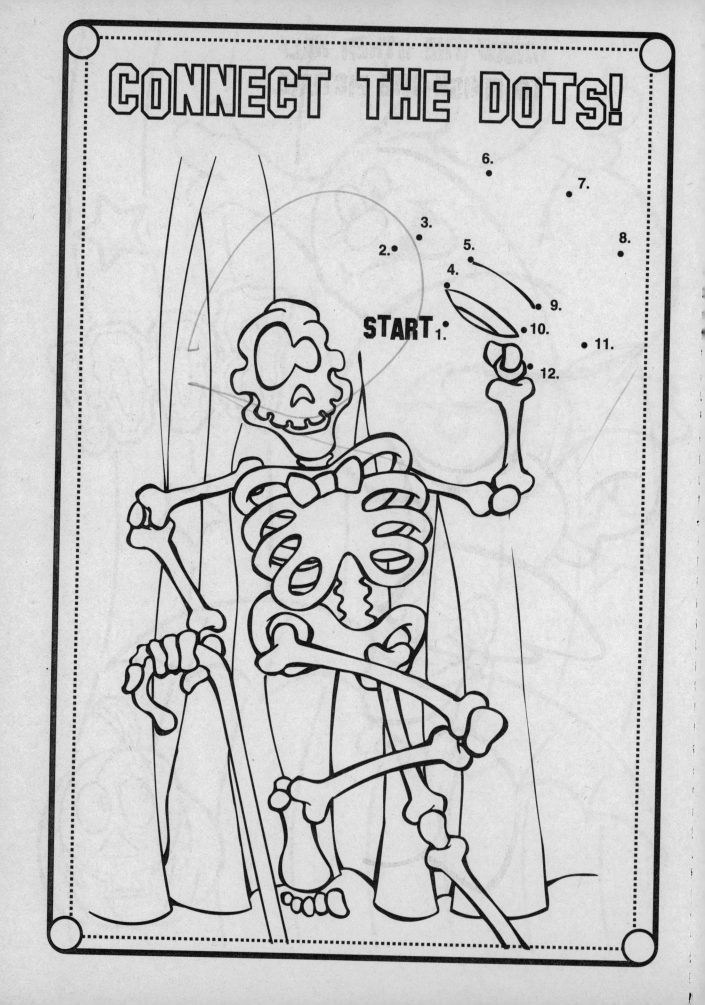

DRAW THE OTHER HALF
TO FINISH THE PICTURE.

Using the letters inside the star, how many words can you find? The object is to create as many words as you can by using adjoining letters. Letters may join: vertically, horizontally, diagonally, left to right, right to left, or up and down.

EXAMPLE:

L	O	O	T	U	N
L	O	F	A	I	L
M	I	V	H	T	E
E	I	S	E	R	A
E	I	L	O	A	D
R	T	E	G	U	Y

TOOL
OFF
RIGHT
TEAR
LOAD

Letter JuGGle

R	O	B	O	T	S
E	R	W	L	O	L
T	A	K	E	T	V
U	E	R	A	R	E
R	U	E	R	U	N
N	S	E	L	A	T

Write words you find on the lines below!

_____
_____
_____
_____
_____
_____
_____
_____

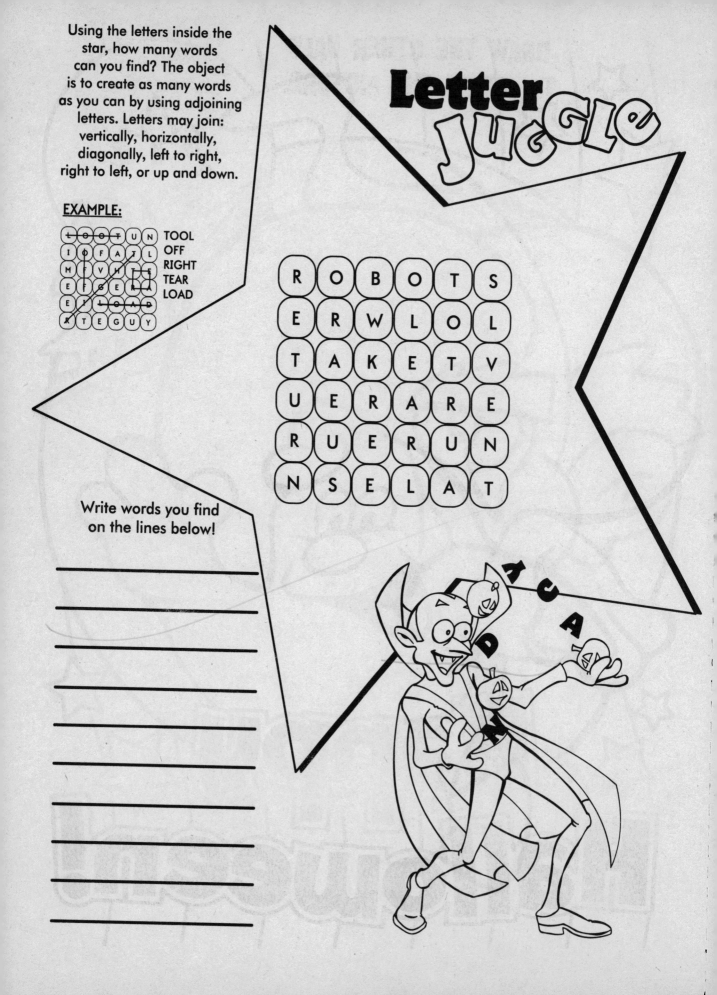

HOW MANY WORDS ABOUT HALLOWEEN CAN YOU FIND IN THE PUZZLE?

APPLES
GOURDS
TREATS
COSTUME

PARADE
WITCH
SCARECROW
TRICKS

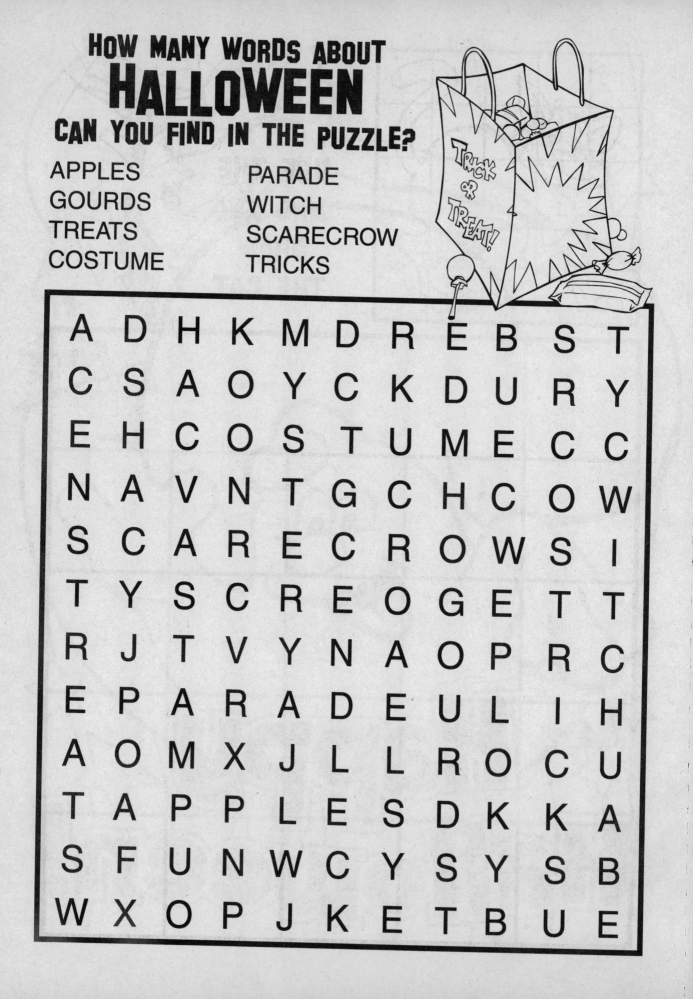

```
A D H K M D R E B S T
C S A O Y C K D U R Y
E H C O S T U M E C C
N A V N T G C H C O W
S C A R E C R O W S I
T Y S C R E O G E T T
R J T V Y N A O P R C
E P A R A D E U L I H
A O M X J L L R O C U
T A P P L E S D K K A
S F U N W C Y S Y S B
W X O P J K E T B U E
```

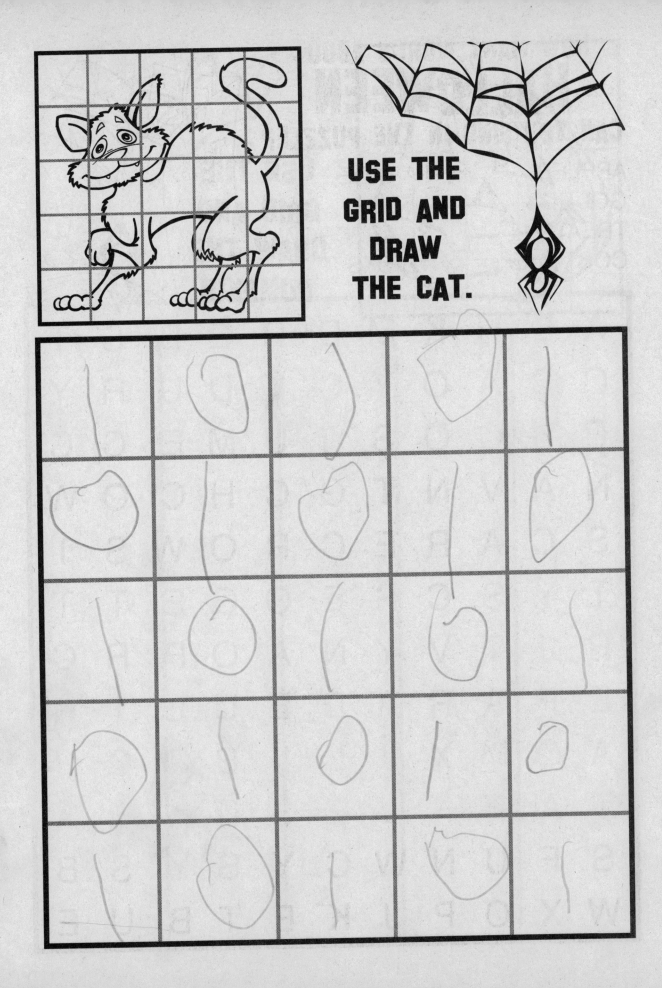

USE THE
GRID AND
DRAW
THE CAT.

USE THE GRID AND DRAW THE PUMPKIN.

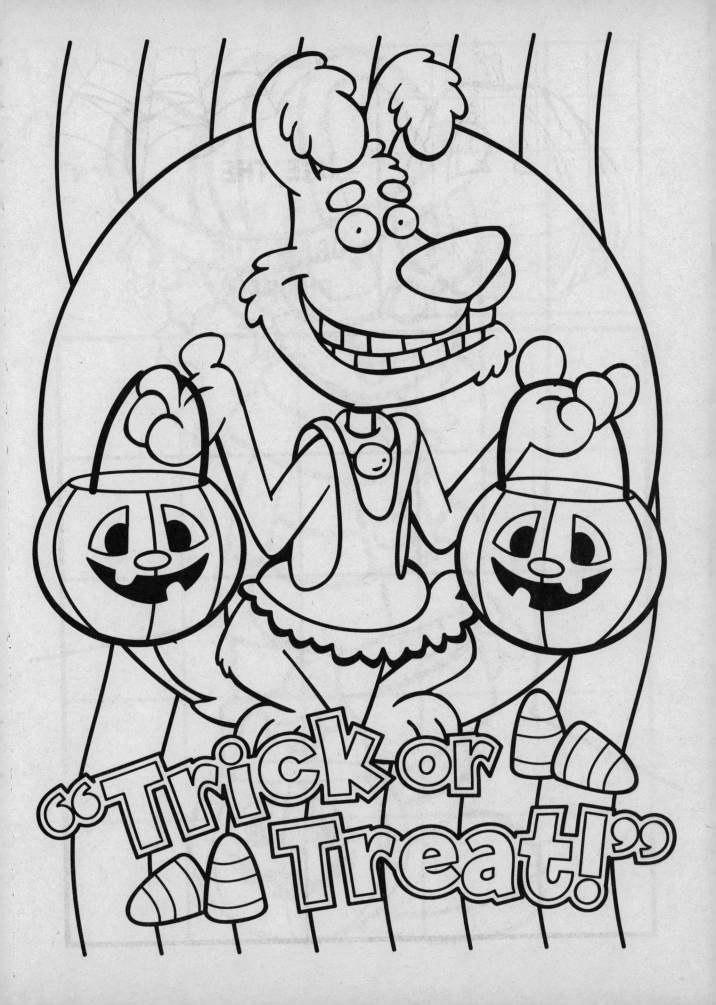

HOW MANY WORDS ABOUT
HALLOWEEN
CAN YOU FIND IN THE PUZZLE?

PARTY   CANDY
HAYRIDE   COSTUME
FUN   CIDER
TREAT   DONUT

```
A D H K M D R E B S T
C S A O Y M I D F R Y
A H A Y R I D E H C C
N A V N T G C H C O D
D T L E T R E A T S O
Y Y S C R E O H E T N
E J T V Y N A C P U U
I P A R T Y I I L M T
J O M X J L L D O E U
P Q D E V O B E K O A
A F U N W C Y R Y E B
W X O P J K E T B U E
```